BASS RECORDED VERSIONS

SUBLIME FOR BASS

Transcriptions by Joe Collinson and Jeff Jacobson

ISBN 978-1-70514-205-9

Visit Hal Leonard Online at
www.halleonard.com

Contact us:
Hal Leonard
7777 West Bluemound Road
Milwaukee, WI 53213
Email: info@halleonard.com

In Europe, contact:
Hal Leonard Europe Limited
42 Wigmore Street
Marylebone, London, W1U 2RN
Email: info@halleonardeurope.com

In Australia, contact:
Hal Leonard Australia Pty. Ltd.
4 Lentara Court
Cheltenham, Victoria, 3192 Australia
Email: info@halleonard.com.au

from Sublime - *Sublime*

April 29, 1992 (Miami)

Words and Music by Brad Nowell, Lawrence Krsone Parker, Marshall Goodman and Mike Happoldt

*Synth bass arr. for bass.

**1st time, sung behind the beat.

1. A - pril twen-ty-six, nine-teen-nine-ty-two, there was a ri - ot on the streets. Tell me, where were you?
   turn _ to the pad to un-load ev-'ry-thing, it dawned on me that I need new home fur-nish-ings. So once a-

You were sit-tin' home, watch-in' your T. V., while I was par-tic-i-pat-in' in some an-ar-chy.
gain we filled the van _ un-til it was full. Since that day, my liv-ing room's been much more com-f'ta-ble. 'Cause ev-'ry-

1st time, Bass 2: w/ Bass Fig. 2 (2 times)
2nd time, Bass 2: w/ Bass Fig. 2 (3 times)

D

First spot we hit, it was my liq-uor store. I fi-nal-ly got all that al-co-hol I can't af-ford. With
bod-y in the hood has had it up to here. It's get-ting hot-ter and hot-ter and har-der each and ev-'ry year. Some

A

red lights flash-in', time to re-tire, and then we turned that liq-uor store in-to a struc-ture fire.
kids went in a store with their moth-er. I saw her when she came out; she was get-tin' some Pam-pers.

D

Next stop we hit, it was the mu-sic shop. It on-ly took one brick to make that win-dow drop.
They said it was for the black man, they said it was for the Mex-i-can, and not for the white man. But if you

To Coda ⊕

A

Fi-nal-ly, we got our own P. A. Where do you think I got this gui-tar that you're hear-in' to-day? Ay!
look at the street, it was-n't a-bout Rod-ney King. Got this fucked-up sit-u-a-tion and these fucked-up po-lice. It's a-

Interlude

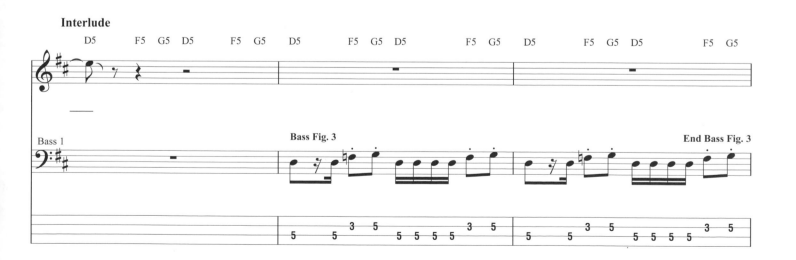

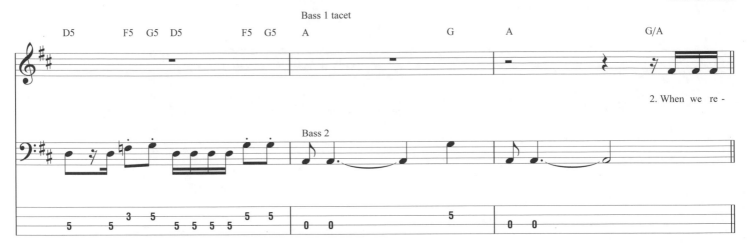

2. When we re -

Coda

bout com-in' up, ___ and stay-in' on top, ___ and scream-in' one-eight-sev-en on a moth-er-fuck-in' ___ cop.

It's not in a pa-per, it's on the wall. Na-tion-al Guard, ___ smoke from all a-round!

Interlude

Bass 1: w/ Bass Fig. 3 (2 times)
w/ Voc. ad lib., next 6 meas.

Bass 1: w/ Bass Fig. 1 (3 times)

Verse

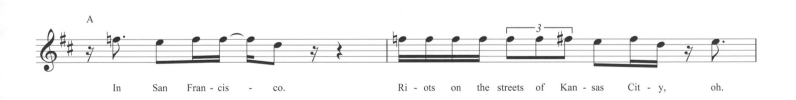

re - ka, Cal - i - for - nia.   Hes - per - i - a.   San - ta Bar - b'ra.   Win - ne - muc - ca, Ne-

(Oh, let it burn, let it burn, let it burn.   Won't you let it burn,   won't you won't you let it burn. ____

Bass 2

Bass 2: w/ Bass Fig. 2 (last 2 meas.)

va - da. Phoe - nix, Ar - i - zo - na. ____ San Di - e - go.   Lake - land, Flor - i - da. ____ Fuck - in', Twen - ty - nine Palms. _

Let it burn. _____ Won't you let it burn? Won't you let it burn, ____ let it

Outro

Bass 2 tacet

D5   F5 G5 D5   F5 G5 D5   F5 G5 D5   F5 G5 D5   F5 G5 D5   F5 G5

burn?) _

Bass 2   Bass 1

D5   F5   G5   D5   F5   G5   D5

from Sublime - *40oz. to Freedom*

Badfish

Words and Music by Brad Nowell

Intro

Verse

Creep and crawl, I step in - to the night.

Pre-Chorus

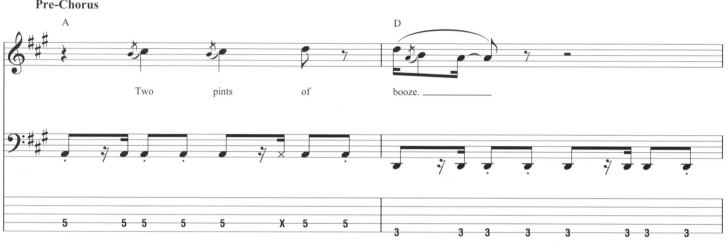

Two pints of booze.

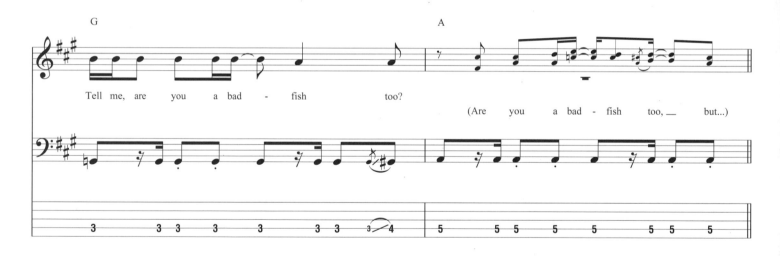

Tell me, are you a bad - fish too?

(Are you a bad - fish too, but...)

Chorus

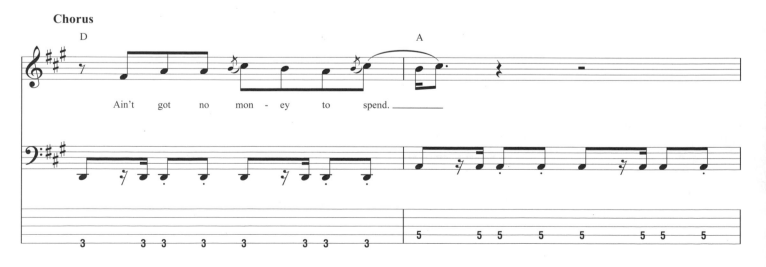

Ain't got no mon - ey to spend.

I hope the night _____ will nev - er end.

Lord _____ knows I'm _____ weak. _____ Won't some -

bod - y get me off of this reef?

Verse

2. Ba - by, you're a big blue whale. _____

let ring - - - - - - - -

Grab the reef ___ when all ___ duck div - ing ___ fails. I

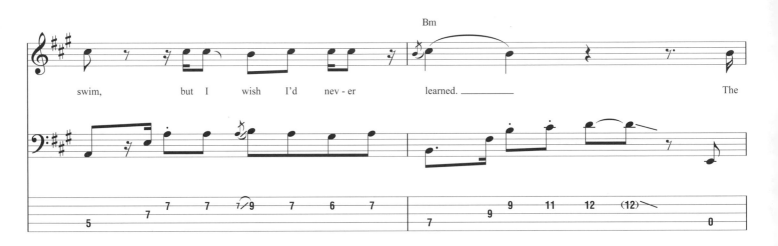

swim, but I wish I'd nev - er learned. ___ The

wat - er's too pol - lu - ted with germs. I

Pre-Chorus

dive deep when it's ten feet o - ver - head. ___

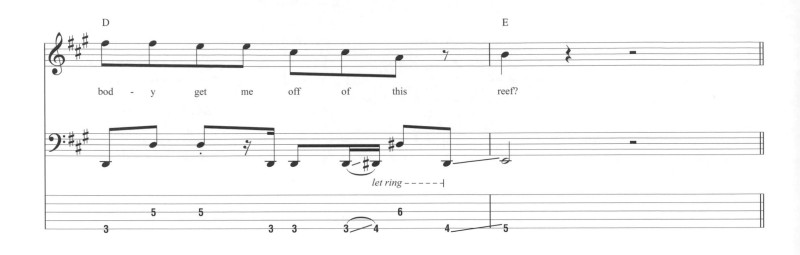

bod - y get me off of this reef?

Interlude

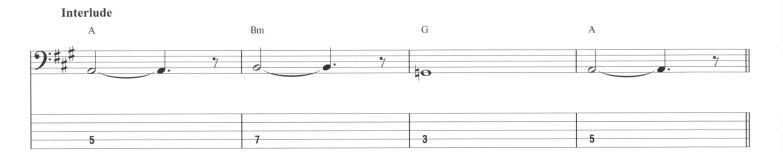

Guitar Solo

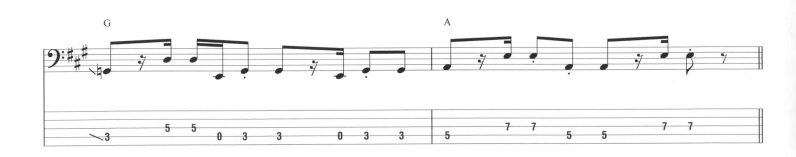

Chorus

Ain't got no quar - rels with God. _____

Ain't got no time _____ to get old. _____

Lord _____ knows I'm _____ weak. _____ Won't some -

bod - y get me off of this reef?

Caress Me Down

Words and Music by Brad Nowell, Eric Wilson and Floyd Gaugh

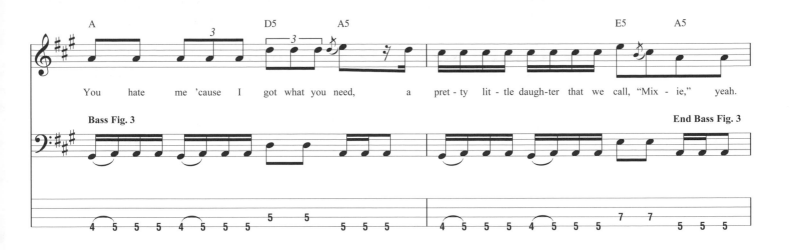

You hate me 'cause I got what you need, a pret-ty lit-tle daugh-ter that we call, "Mix-ie," yeah.

If you wan-na get beat phy-si-c'ly, it will be o-ver in a min-ute if ya... 2. So she

Verse

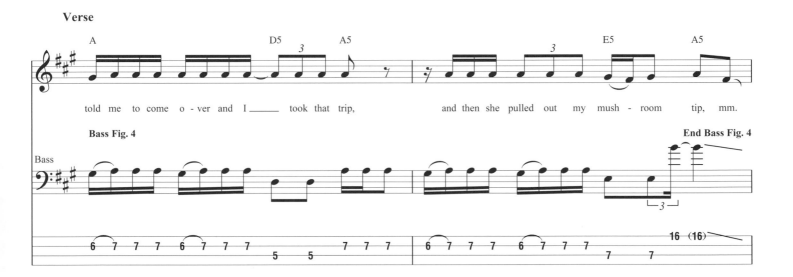

told me to come o-ver and I ___ took that trip, and then she pulled out my mush-room tip, mm.

And when it came out it went drip, drip, drip. I did-n't know she had the G. I. Joe kung fu grip. And it went,

Chorus

Uh, and the girl ca-ress me down. Uh, and that's that lov-in' sound. And it went

Verse

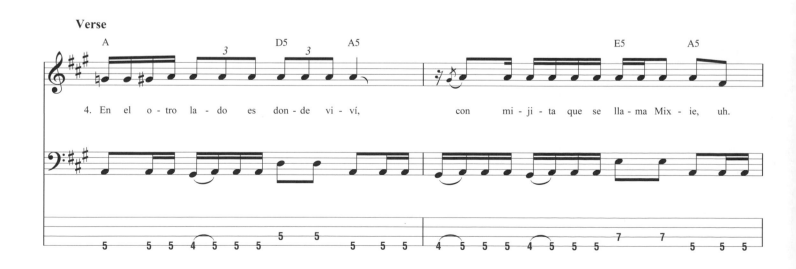

Su her-man-a sí ___ me quie-re y a-ho-ri-ta te-ne-mos un be-bé. Sus

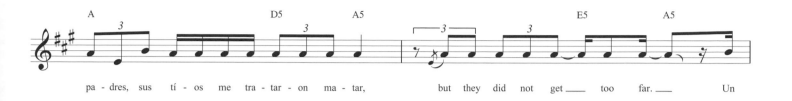

pa-dres, sus tí-os me tra-tar-on ma-tar, but they did not get ___ too far. ___ Un

po-co des-pués, tu-ve que re-gre-sar con un chin-go de di-ner-o, 'cause you know I'm a star. Mi

fui a Cos-ta Ri-ca pa-ra to-mar y su-pe-ar, pla-ti-ca-ba con la ra-za, 'cause they know who we are. Si

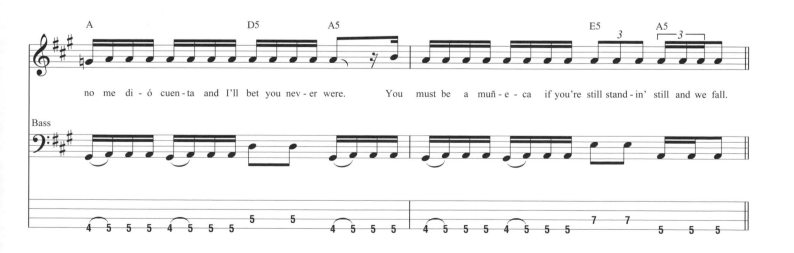

no me di-ó cuen-ta and I'll bet you nev-er were. You must be a muñ-e-ca if you're still stand-in' still and we fall.

Chorus

Bass: w/ Bass Fig. 5

Uh, and the girl ca - ress me down. Uh, and that's the lov - in' sound. We go

Uh, and the girl ca - ress me down, and that's the lov - in' ____ sound.

Interlude

Bass: w/ Bass Fig. 1

5. Me

Verse

Bass: w/ Bass Fig. 4 (1st 2 meas.)

gus - ta mi reg - gae, me gus - ta punk rock. Pe - ro la co - sa que me gus - ta más es pan - o - chi - ta. A

nal - ga en el air - e if you know who you are. Pon la nal - ga en el air - e, em - pi - e - za gri - tar.

Bass

Bass: w/ Bass Fig. 3 (2 times)

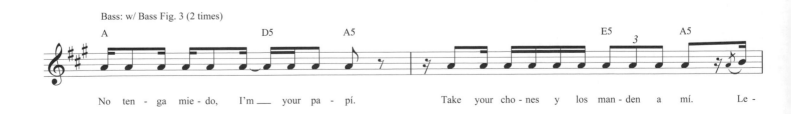

No ten - ga mie - do, I'm ____ your pa - pí. Take your cho - nes y los man - den a mí. Le -

van - ta, le - van - ta, ti - en - es que gri - tar. Le - van - ta, le - van - ta, ti - en - es que bai - lar. 'Cause...

Chorus

Bass: w/ Bass Fig. 5

Uh, and the girl ca - ress me down. Uh, and that's the lov - in' sound.

Uh, and the girl ca - ress me down. That's the lov - in' _____ sound. _____

Chorus

Bass: w/ Bass Fig. 5

_____ Uh, ca - ress me down. Uh, that's the lov - in' sound, uh.

Outro

*Sing 1st time only.

Date Rape

Words and Music by Brad Nowell

Tune up 1/4 step

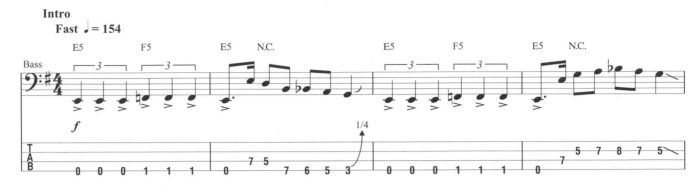

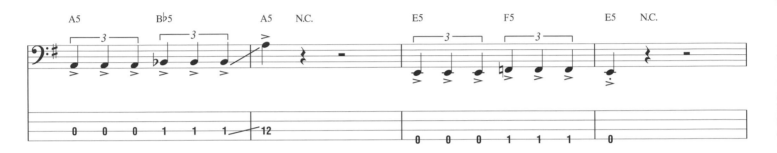

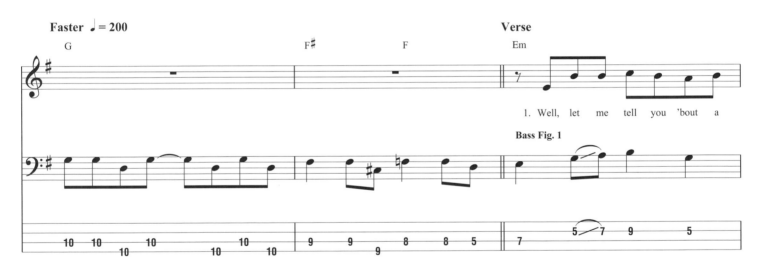

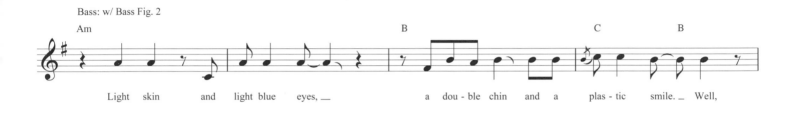

"Wait a min-ute, I have to think." __ He said, ___"That's fine. __ May I please buy you a drink?" __

One drink turned in-to three or four ___ and they left and got in-to his car. __

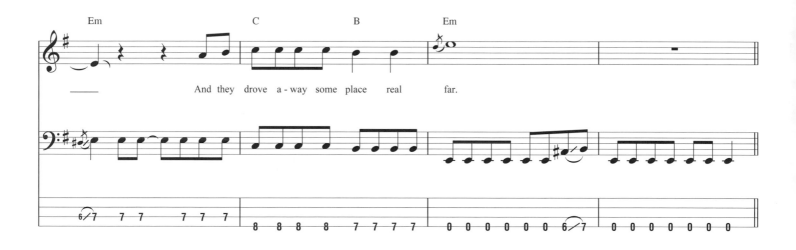

___ And they drove a-way some place real far.

Pre-Chorus

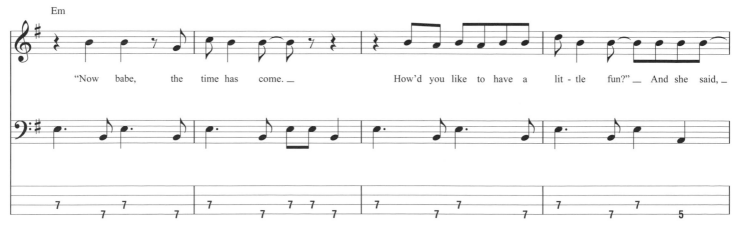

"Now babe, the time has come. __ How'd you like to have a lit-tle fun?" __ And she said,

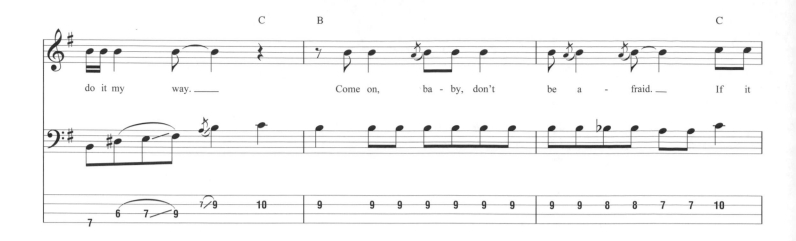

do it my way. ___   Come on,   ba - by, don't   be a - fraid. ___   If it

Freely   **A tempo**

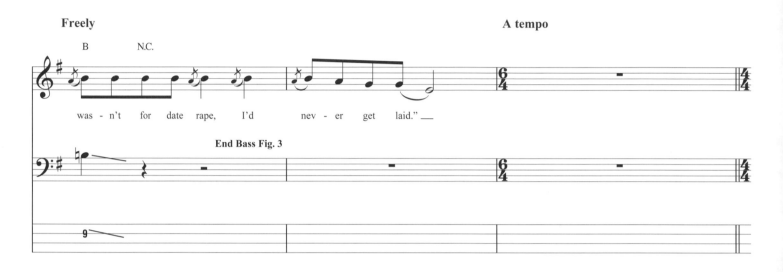

was - n't   for date rape,   I'd   nev - er   get   laid." ___

End Bass Fig. 3

Guitar Solo

Bass: w/ Bass Fig. 1 (2 times)

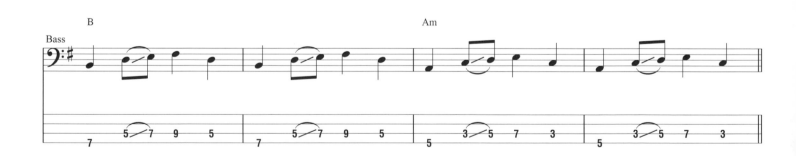

Interlude
Tempo I

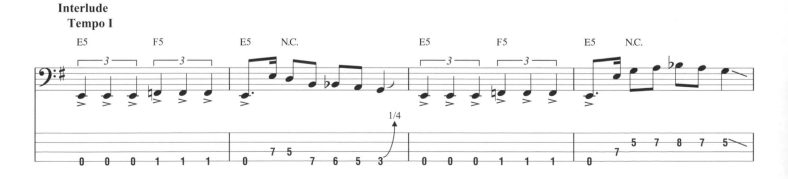

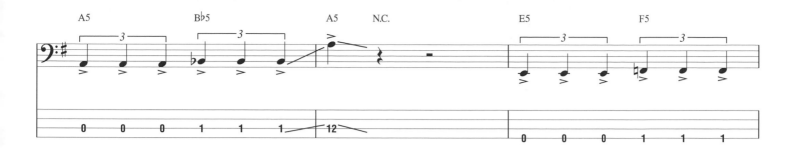

Tempo II

Verse

Bass: w/ Bass Fig. 1

2. He fin-ished up, he start-ed the car. ___ He turned a-round and drove back to the bar. ___

Bass: w/ Bass Fig. 2

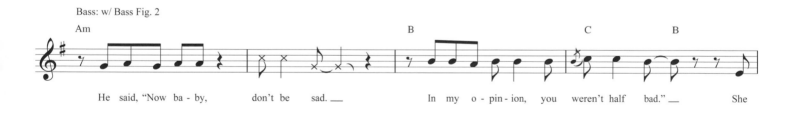

He said, "Now ba-by, don't be sad. ___ In my o-pin-ion, you weren't half bad." ___ She

picked up a rock, threw it at the car. Hit him in the head, now he's got a big scar. Come on ___

Bass

you par-ty peo-ple, won't you lis-ten to me? Date rape sty - lee.

Verse

Bass: w/ Bass Fig. 1

3. The next day she went to her drawer, __ looked up her lo - cal at - tor-ney at law. __

Went to the phone and filed a po-lice re-port, __ and then she took the guy's ass to court. __ Well,

the day he stood in front of the judge __ he screamed, __ "She lies, __ that lit-tle __ slut!" __

That's when things got out of con - trol. The

Chorus

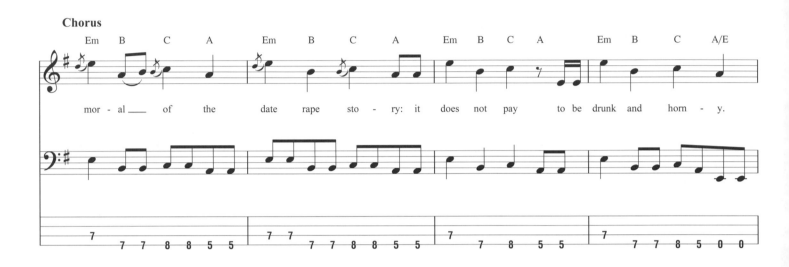

mor - al ___ of the date rape sto - ry: it does not pay to be drunk and horn - y.

Bass: w/ Bass Fig. 3

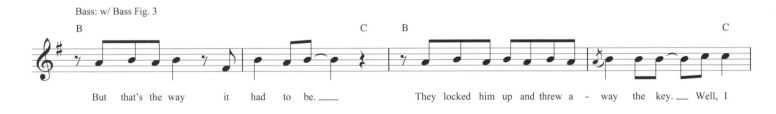

But that's the way it had to be. ___ They locked him up and threw a - way the key. ___ Well, I

Freely

Bass tacet

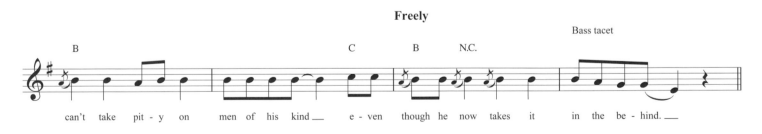

can't take pit - y on men of his kind ___ e - ven though he now takes it in the be - hind. ___

Chorus
A tempo

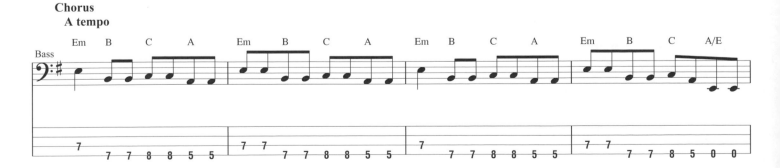

That's the way it had to be. ___ They locked him up and threw a - way the key. ___ Well, I

Can't take pit - y on men of his kind ___ e - ven though he now takes it in the be - hind. ___ Date rape!

Interlude

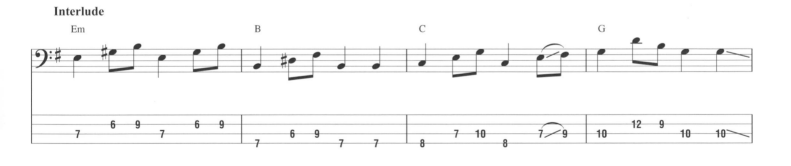

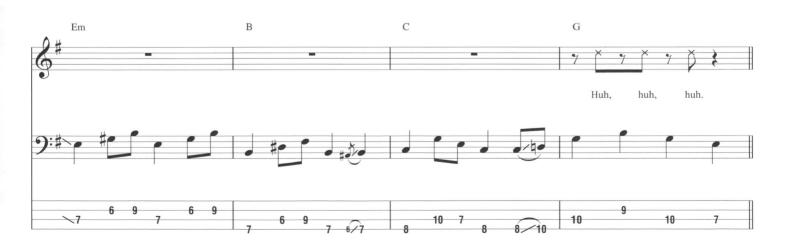

Huh, huh, huh.

from Sublime - *Sublime*
Doin' Time

Words and Music by Brad Nowell, Adam Horovitz, Adam Yauch, Rick Rubin, Marshall Goodman, George Gershwin, Ira Gershwin, DuBose Heyward and Dorothy Heyward

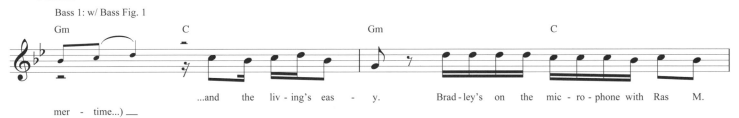

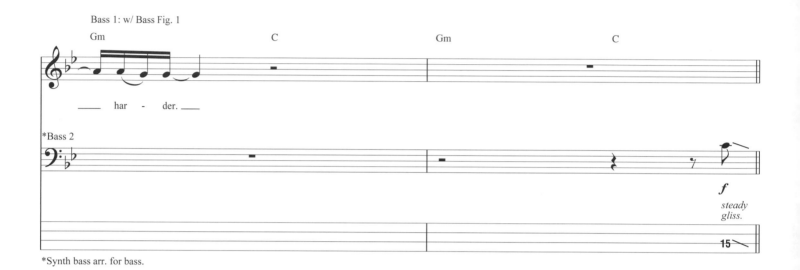

*Synth bass arr. for bass.

Verse

On lock - down like a pen - i - ten - tia - ry, _____ she spreads her

lov - in' all ___ o - ver and when ___ she gets home, _ there's none left ___ for me. _

Bass Fill 1

End Bass Fill 1

Bass 1

steady gliss.

```
10-10      10-13      12      10    13    12
                         10
```

𝄋 Chorus

Bass 1: w/ Bass Fig. 2 (2 times)
Bass 2: w/ Bass Fig. 4 (2 times)

...and the liv - in's eas - y. Brad - ley's on the mi - cro - phone with Ras M.

(Sum - mer - time...) _____

G. All the peo - ple in the dance will a - gree that we're well - qual - i - fied to rep - re - sent the L. B.

Bass 1: w/ Bass Fig. 3

C. { Me and me and Lou - ie, _____ we go } run to the par - ty and dance to the rhy - thm, it
  { G, me and Lou - ie, _____ }

Bass 2   Bass Fig. 5

End Bass Fig. 5

```
        3   5    5         5
3            3                    0  0    0   0
                       1              2    2    2    2
```

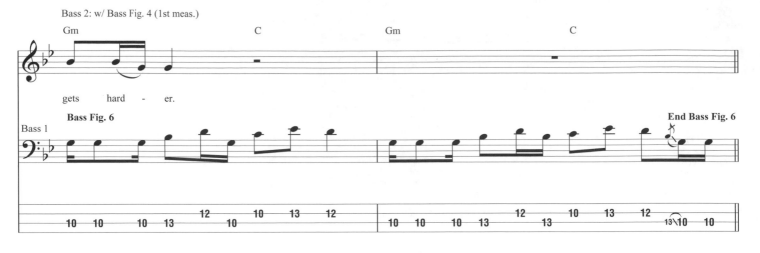

Verse

*Chord symbols reflect implied harmony.

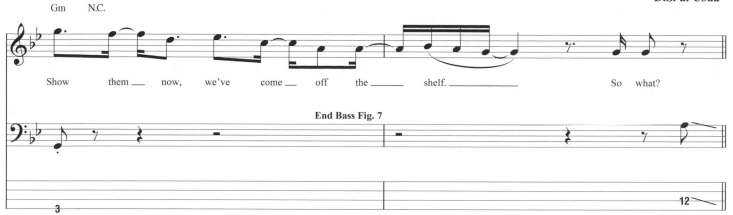

Show them __ now, we've come __ off the __ shelf. _____ So what?

End Bass Fig. 7

⊕ Coda

Verse

Bass 2: w/ Bass Fig. 4 (4 times)
Bass 1 tacet

3. E - vil. I've come to tell you that she's e - vil, most def - i - nite - ly.

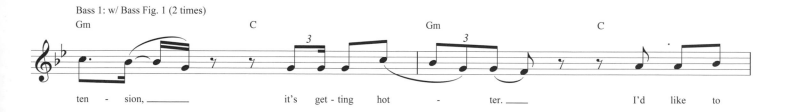

E - vil. Or - n'ry, scan - dal - ous and e - vil, most def - i - nite - ly. The

Bass 1: w/ Bass Fig. 1 (2 times)

ten - sion, _____ it's get - ting hot - ter. ____ I'd like to

hold __ her ____ head un - der - wa - ter. ____ Oh, oh, oh, oh, oh, oh.

Bridge

Bass 2: w/ Bass Fig. 4 (2 times)

Me and my girl, we got a re-la-

-tion - ship, __ huh. And me and my _____ girl, _____ hmm, __ we got a re-la-

Bass 2: w/ Bass Fig. 7

-tion - ship. __ Mm - hmm. My girl, _____ we got a re-la-

Bass 2: w/ Bass Fill 1

-tion - ship. __ Oh. _____ And my _____ girl, _____ yeah, we got a re-la-
(Take a

Chorus

Bass 1: w/ Bass Fig. 2 (2 times)
Bass 2: w/ Bass Fig. 4 (2 times)

Brad-ley's on the mi - cro-phone with Ras M.

-tion - ship. __
tip, take a tip, take a ti - ti - ti-tip from me.) ___

G. All the peo-ple in the dance will a - gree that we're __ well - qual - i - fied to rep - re - sent the L. B.

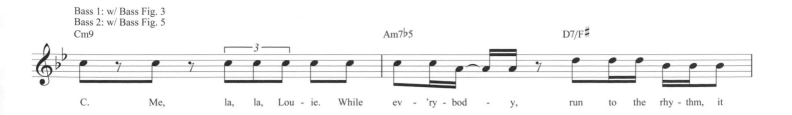

Bass 1: w/ Bass Fig. 3
Bass 2: w/ Bass Fig. 5

Cm9 ... Am7♭5 ... D7/F♯

C. Me, la, la, Lou - ie. While ev - 'ry-bod - y, run to the rhy - thm, it

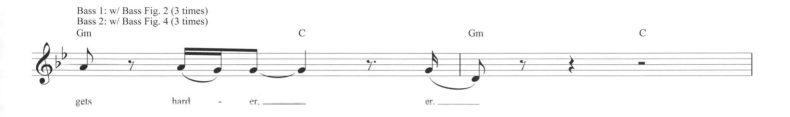

Bass 1: w/ Bass Fig. 2 (3 times)
Bass 2: w/ Bass Fig. 4 (3 times)

Gm ... C ... Gm ... C

gets hard - er, _____ er. _____

Gm ... C ... Gm ... C

...and the liv - in's eas - y.

(Sum - mer - time...) _____

Bass 1: w/ Bass Fig. 3
Bass 2: w/ Bass Fig. 5

Gm ... C ... Gm ... C ... Cm9

Bass 1: w/ Bass Fig. 7
Bass 2: w/ Bass Fig. 4 (1st meas.)

Am7♭5 ... D7/F♯ ... Gm ... C ... Gm ... C

Outro

Bass 1: w/ Bass Fig. 1 (2 times)
Bass 2: w/ Bass Fig. 4 (2 times)

Repeat & fade

Gm ... C ... Gm ... C ... Gm ... C ... Gm ... C

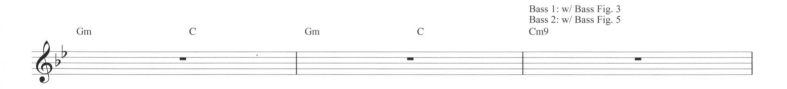

Ebin

Words and Music by Brad Nowell

Spoken: You can hear the fuckin' fleas crawlin' on my nuts.

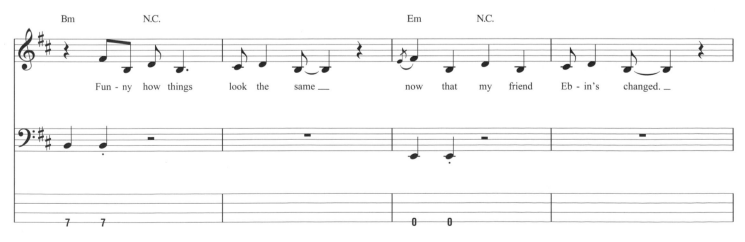

Chorus

Eb - in, you _____ changed. _____

Bass: w/ Bass Fig. 1 (last 4 meas.)

Eb - in, Eb - in, Eb - in, Eb - in, you... _____ Oh, how _____ you changed. _____

Interlude

Oh, _____ you changed. _____

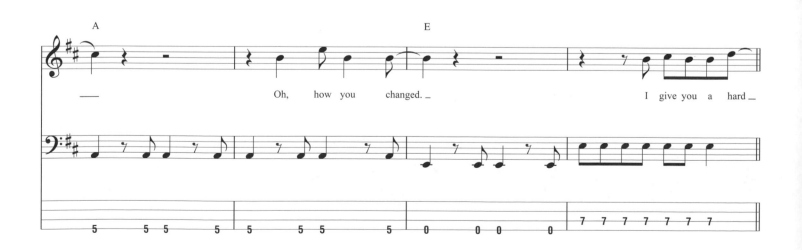

Oh, how you changed. _____ I give you a hard _____

Bridge

Verse

2. Hooked on crack just the oth-er day. ___ Now he's down with the C I A. ___ We got

co-vert op-er-a-tions in Vi-et-nam. ___ Played a hit-man as-sas-sin, like the law's long arm. ___

Bass: w/ Bass Fig. 1 (1st 6 meas.)

He went there to pro-tect his coun-try, eat Mex-i-can food and make

lots of mon-ey. ___ Come back ___ up north, ___ drive a big white car, ___ and

take him-self a plane down to Ni-ca-ra-gua. Well, it feels ___ like I'm the on-ly one ___ to blame. ___

Bridge

time. ___ I did-n't wan-na stay. ___ You got out of jail ___ just the ver-y next day. ___

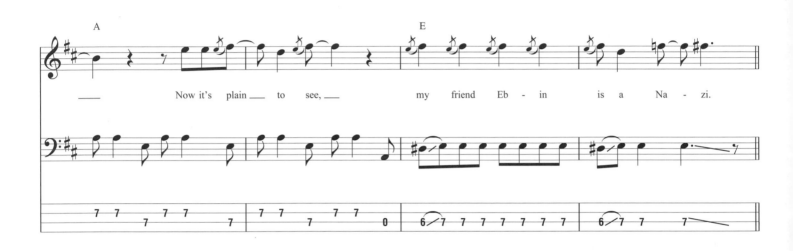

___ Now it's plain ___ to see, ___ my friend Eb - in is a Na - zi.

Guitar Solo

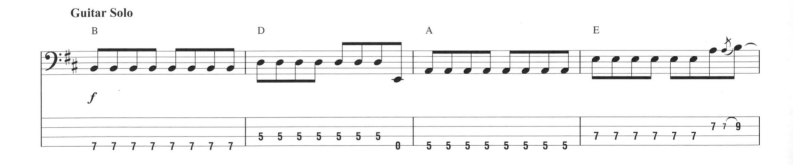

Bass: w/ Bass Fig. 1

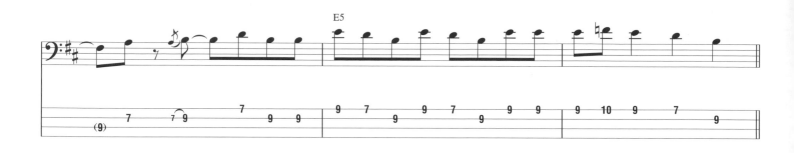

Verse

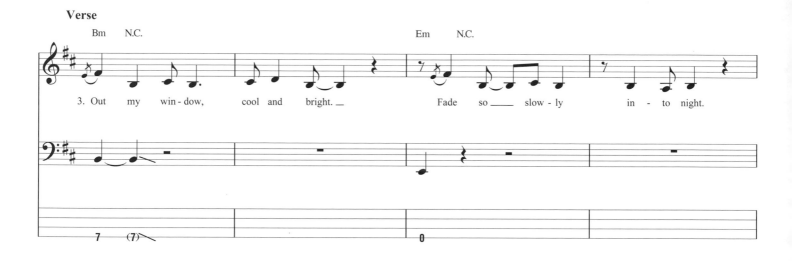

3. Out my win-dow, cool and bright. __ Fade so __ slow-ly in - to night.

Fun - ny how things look the same __ now that my friend Eb - in's changed. __

Outro

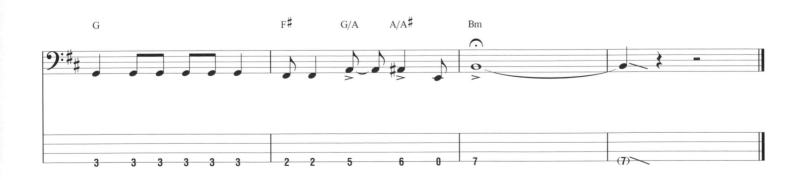

40 Oz. to Freedom

Words and Music by Brad Nowell

*Chord symbols reflect implied harmony.

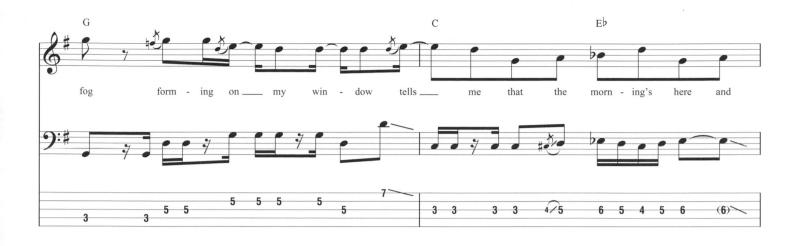

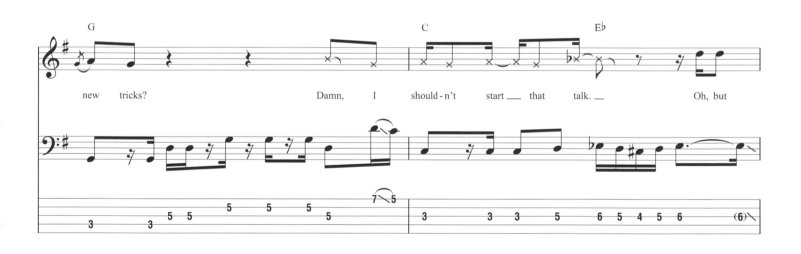

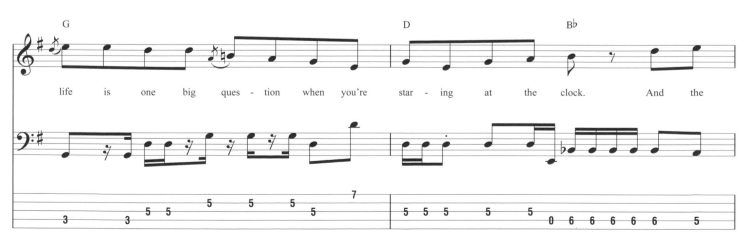

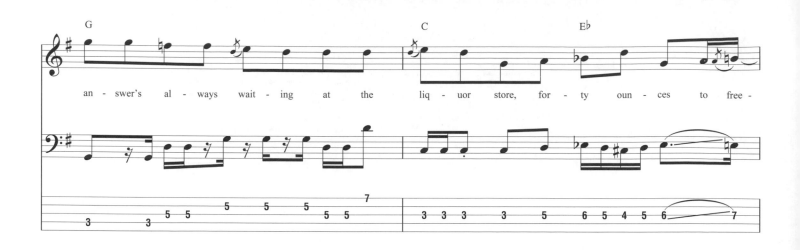

Chorus

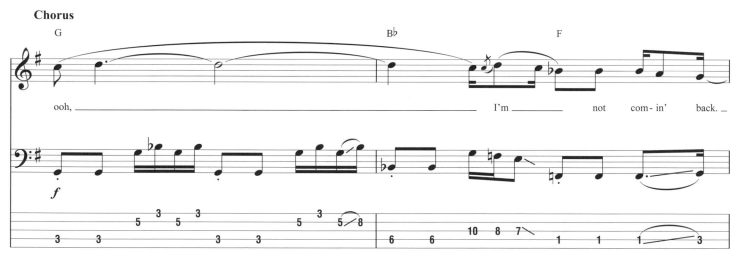

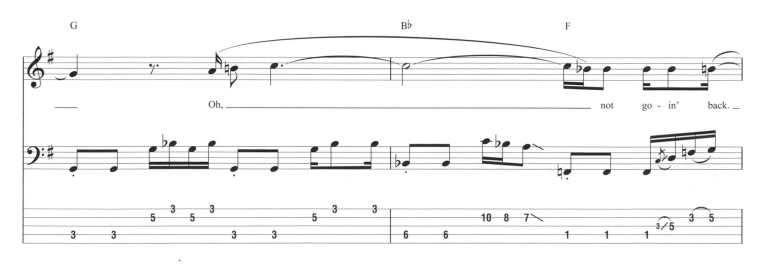

Oh, _____ God _____ knows _____ I'm not go-in' back. _____

Oh, _____ I'm not go-in'. _____

Interlude

Spoken: Hey man, does anyone make a run down to AMPM with me?

It's like, quarter to

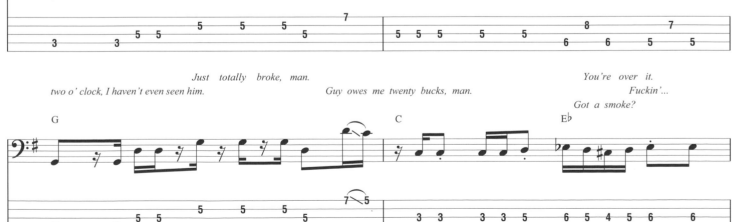

Could you like um, loan me like a buck or two dude? Um, *I'm totally broke right now.*
two right now my bro, let's skate. *Chai should...* *Chai said he was gonna be here at like*

Just totally broke, man. *You're over it.*
two o' clock, I haven't even seen him. *Guy owes me twenty bucks, man.* *Fuckin'...*
Got a smoke?

Interlude

Outro-Chorus

from Sublime - *Sublime*

Garden Grove

Words and Music by Brad Nowell, Eric Wilson, Floyd Gaugh and Linton Johnson

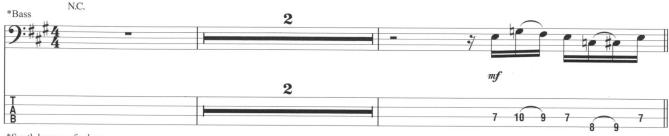

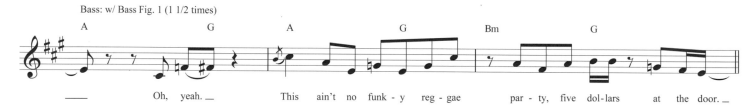

Bridge

Verse

Interlude

Pawn Shop

Words and Music by Brad Nowell, Eric Wilson, Floyd Gaugh, Winston Matthews and Lloyd MacDonald

*Chord symbols reflect implied harmony.

Down {there/here} at the pawn shop, it's {the way, on-ly/a dif-f'rent} way to shop. Down {there/here} at the pawn shop, {if it's not in stone./it's a-noth-er sold.} Down {there/here} at the pawn shop, {ain't no way, no way to shop./it's some'n' if you nev-er shop}

Verse

Down {there/down here} at the pawn shop. 1. What has been ___ told?

Al - bi - no made of stone. But just re-mem-ber that it's flesh and bone. ___

Interlude

Bass: w/ Bass Fig. 1

Bass: w/ Bass Fig. 1 (1st meas.)

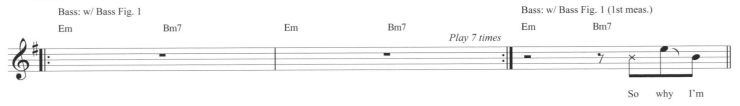

Play 7 times

So why I'm

Chorus

Bass: w/ Bass Fig. 1 (4 times)

down here at the pawn shop. Down here at the pawn shop.

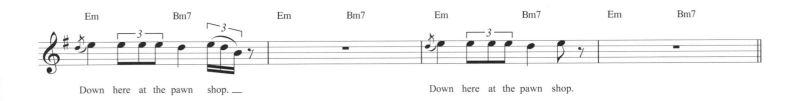

Down here at the pawn shop. ___ Down here at the pawn shop.

Verse

Bass: w/ Bass Fig. 1 (4 times)

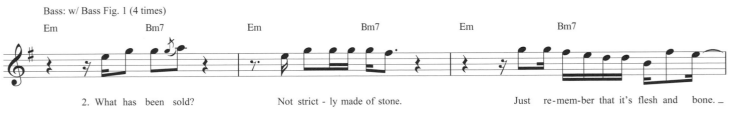

2. What has been sold? Not strict - ly made of stone. Just re-mem-ber that it's flesh and bone. ___

___ And I have heard, light like ___ a bird. _____

Chorus

Bass: w/ Bass Fig. 1 (2 times)

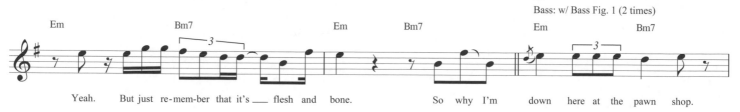

Yeah. But just re-mem-ber that it's ___ flesh and bone. So why I'm down here at the pawn shop.

Down here at the pawn shop.

Interlude

Bass: w/ Bass Fig. 1

Bass: w/ Bass Fig. 1 (2 times)

Play 5 times

Go!

D.S. al Coda

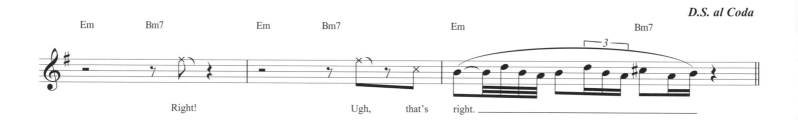

Right! Ugh, that's right. ___

⊕ **Coda**

Verse

Bass: w/ Bass Fig. 1 (4 times)

3. What has been ___ sold? Not strict-ly made of stone. ___

Just re-mem-ber it's flesh and bone. ___ What has been sold?

Not strict - ly soul. __ Please re-mem-ber it's flesh and bone. __ Why I'm

Outro-Chorus

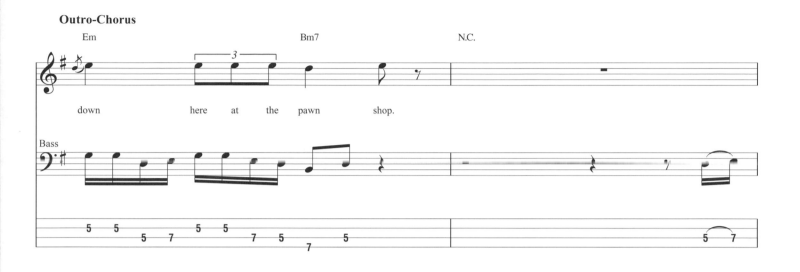

down here at the pawn shop.

Bass

Bass: w/ Bass Fig. 1 (3 times)

Down here at the pawn shop.   Down here at the pawn shop. __

Down here at the pawn shop, yop, yop. Huh! Ooh. _

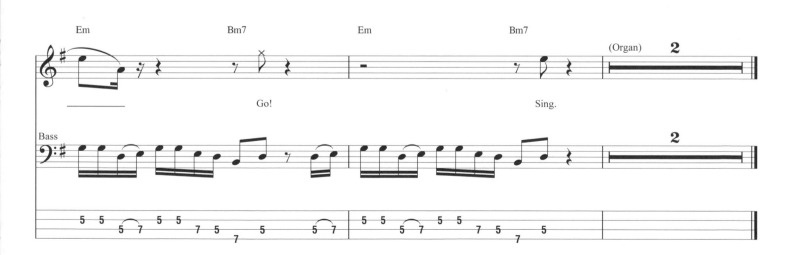

_____   Go!   Sing.

Bass

from Sublime - *Sublime*

Santeria

Words and Music by Brad Nowell, Eric Wilson and Floyd Gaugh

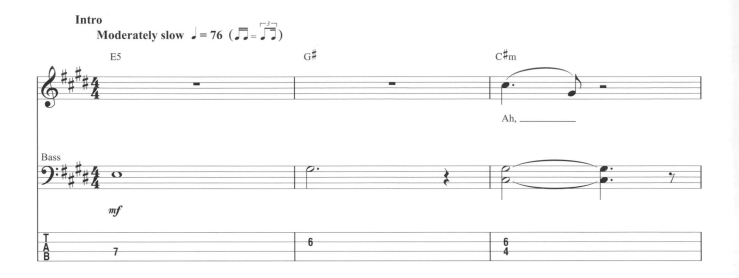

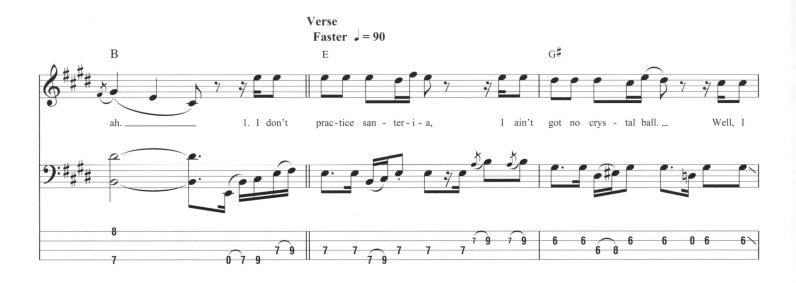

from Sublime - *40oz. to Freedom*

Smoke Two Joints

Words and Music by Chris Kay and Michael Kay

Spoken: *She was living in a single room with three other individuals.*
One of them was a male, and the other two... well, the other two were females.
God only knows what they were up to in there.
And furthermore Susan, I wouldn't be the least bit surprised to learn that all four
of them habitually smoke marijuana cigarettes.
Reefers!

Drop-D tuning:
(low to high) D-A-D-G

Intro

Moderately slow ♩ = 95

Double-time feel

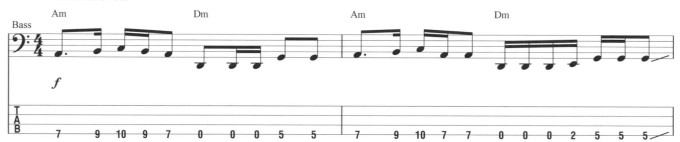

End double-time feel

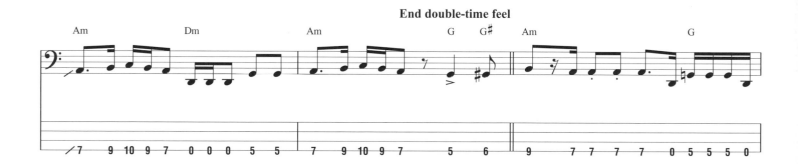

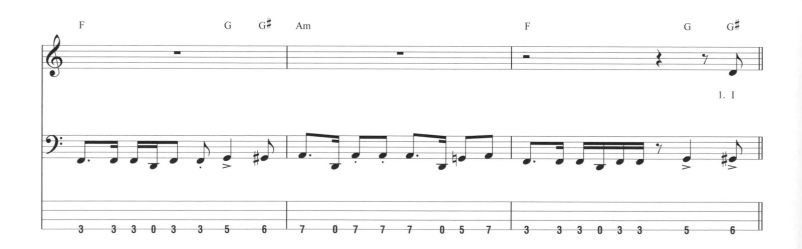

Verse

Interlude

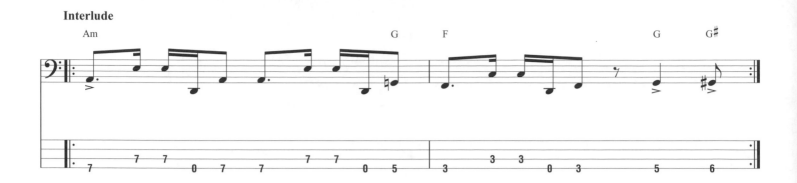

w/ Voc. ad lib., next 8 meas.

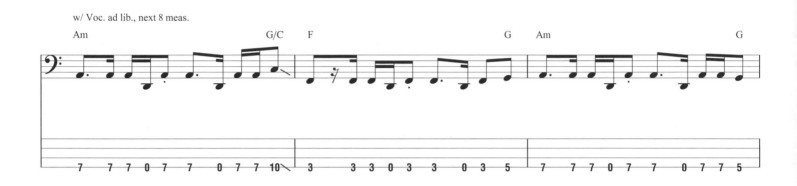

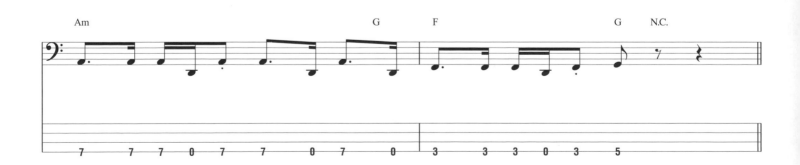

Guitar Solo

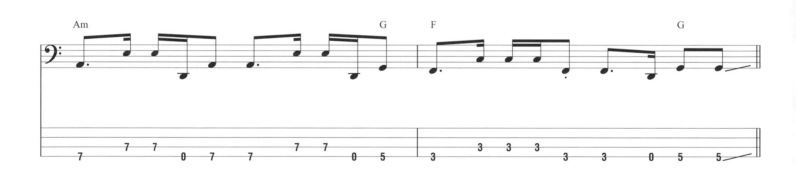

Interlude

Whoa. _____

Bridge

Bass: w/ Bass Fig. 1 (3 times)

A5

Rock me to - night. _____ Whoa. _____ Jah say. _____ Whoa. _

Outro
Double-time feel

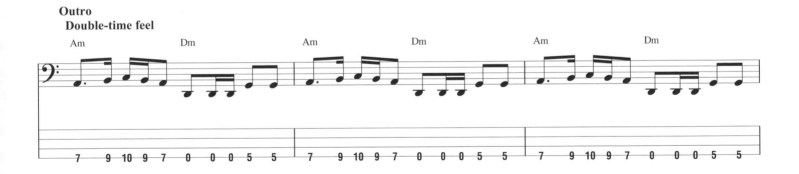

Freely

steady gliss.

from Sublime - *Robbin' the Hood*

STP

Words and Music by Brad Nowell

Spoken: I hope you're recordin' this.

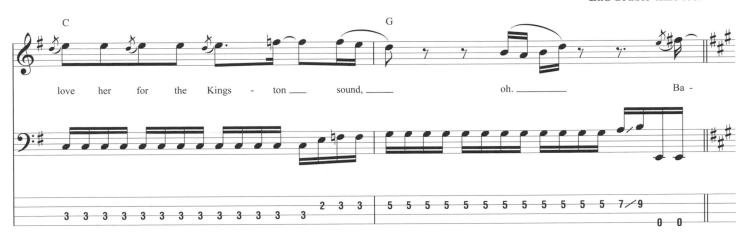

love her for the Kings - ton ___ sound, ___ oh. ___ Ba -

Outro

- by, you wan - na give ___ me kiss - es sweet. ___ On -

Bass Fig. 1   End Bass Fig. 1

Bass: w/ Bass Fig. 1 (3 times)

- ly for a night ___ with no re - peat. ___ Ba - by, you wan - na leave ___ and nev-er go. ___

Freely

___ Oh, but the taste of hon-ey is worse than none ___ at all.

Wrong Way

Words and Music by Brad Nowell, Eric Wilson and Floyd Guagh

We talk all night, try ___ to make it right. Be - lieve me, shit was tight. It was the wrong way. ___

Verse

Bass: w/ Bass Fig. 1

4. Don't run a - way if you wan - na stay, ___ 'cause I ain't here to make ya. Oh, ___ no.

It's up to you what you real - ly wan - na do. Spend some time in A - me - ri - ca. Ha, dub ___ style!

Trombone Solo

w/ Voc. ad lib., next 8 meas.

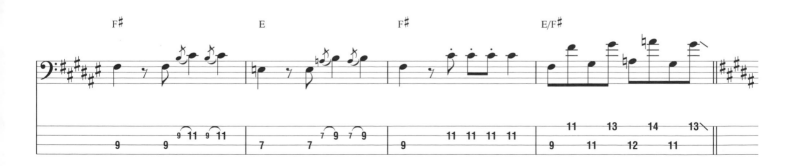

Verse

Bass: w/ Bass Fig. 2

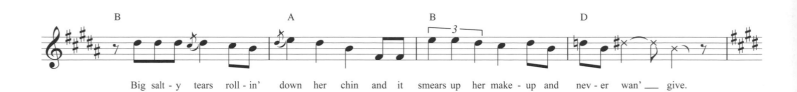

5. She'll give you all that she's got to give, __ but I'm __ gon - na make it hard to live. __

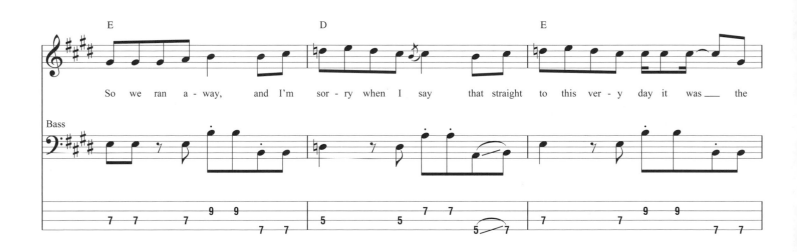

Big salt - y tears roll - in' down her chin and it smears up her make - up and nev - er wan' __ give.

So we ran a - way, and I'm sor - ry when I say that straight to this ver - y day it was __ the

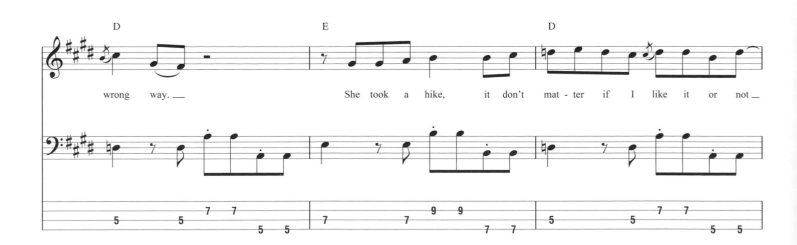

wrong way. __ She took a hike, it don't mat - ter if I like it or not __

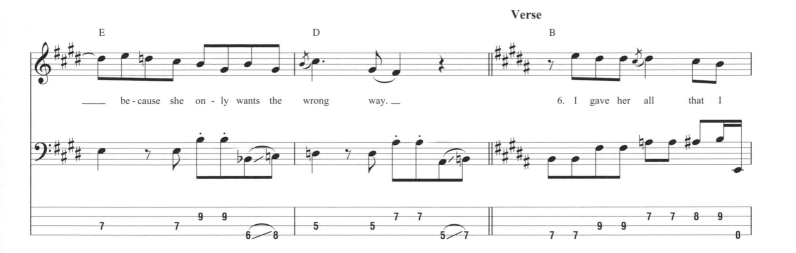

Verse

be - cause she on - ly wants the wrong way. ___ 6. I gave her all that I

had to give, ___ but she still would-n't take it. Whoa, ___ whoa. Her two brown eyes are leak - in'

like a seive ___ and it still ru - ins her make - up and nev - er wan' give.

91

from Sublime - *Sublime*

What I Got

Words and Music by Brad Nowell, Eric Wilson, Floyd Gaugh and Lindon Roberts

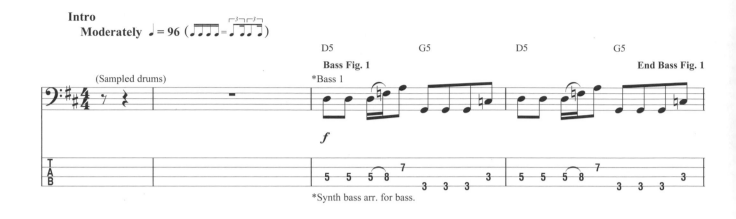

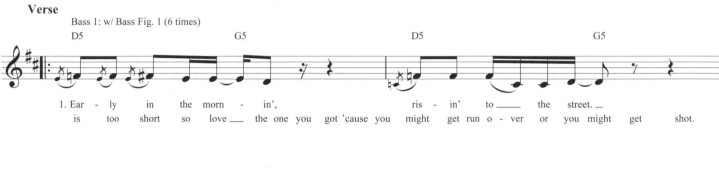

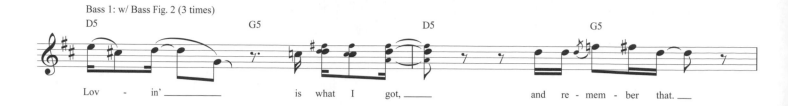

Lov - in' _____ is what I got, _____ and re - mem - ber that. _____

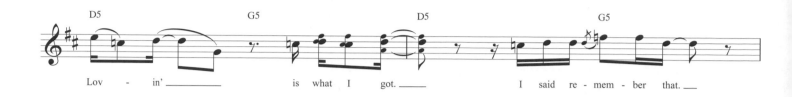

Lov - in' _____ is what I got. _____ I said re - mem - ber that. _____

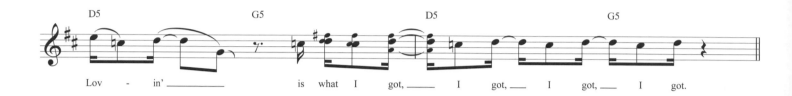

Lov - in' _____ is what I got, _____ I got, ___ I got, ___ I got.

Verse

Bass 1: w/ Bass Fig. 2 (2 1/2 times)

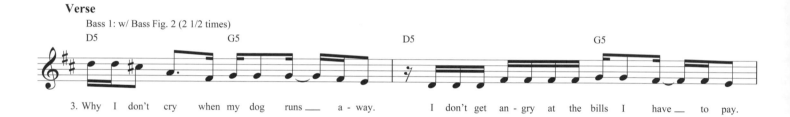

3. Why I don't cry when my dog runs ___ a - way. I don't get an - gry at the bills I have ___ to pay.

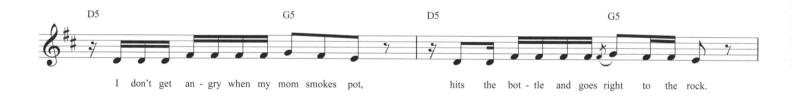

I don't get an - gry when my mom smokes pot, hits the bot - tle and goes right to the rock.

*Bass 1: w/ Bass Fig. 2 (last meas.)

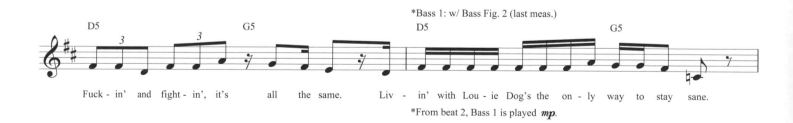

Fuck - in' and fight - in', it's all the same. Liv - in' with Lou - ie Dog's the on - ly way to stay sane.

*From beat 2, Bass 1 is played *mp*.

Bass 1: w/ Bass Fig. 2 (1st meas.)   **Bass 1: w/ Fill 1

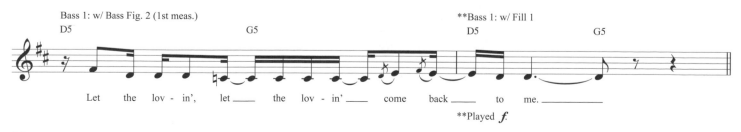

Let the lov - in', let ___ the lov - in' ___ come back ___ to me. _____

**Played *f*.

Interlude

*Upright bass arr. for bass.

'Cause

Chorus

Basses 1 & 2: w/ Bass Figs. 3 & 3A (2 times)

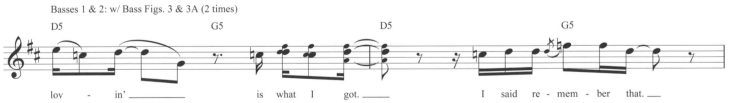

lov - in' _____ is what I got. _____ I said re - mem - ber that. ___

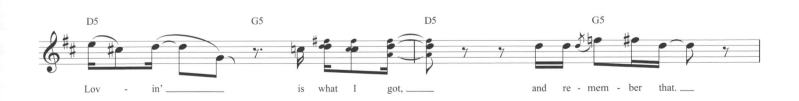

Lov - in' _____ is what I got, _____ and re - mem - ber that. ___

Bass 2: w/ Bass Fig. 3 (2 times)

Lov - in' _____ is what I got, ____ now. I said re - mem - ber that. ___

Lov - in' _____ is what I got, ____ I got, ____ I got, ____ I got.

Outro

Bass 2: w/ Bass Fig. 3

Bass 1 tacet

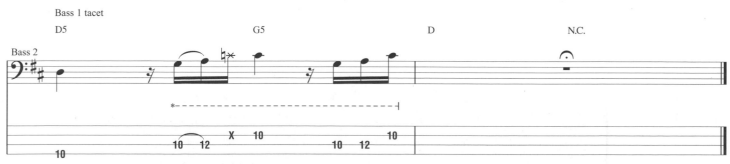

*Played behind the beat.